Editor-in-Chief and Founder:
  *Lyndon H. LaRouche, Jr.*
Editorial Board: *Lyndon H. LaRouche, Jr. , Helga
  Zepp-LaRouche, Robert Ingraham, Tony
  Papert, Gerald Rose, Dennis Small, Jeffrey
  Steinberg, William Wertz*
Co-Editors: *Robert Ingraham, Tony Papert*
Managing Editor: *Nancy Spannaus*
Technology: *Marsha Freeman*
Books: *Katherine Notley*
Ebooks: *Richard Burden*
Graphics: *Alan Yue*
Photos: *Stuart Lewis*
Circulation Manager: *Stanley Ezrol*

INTELLIGENCE DIRECTORS
Counterintelligence: *Jeffrey Steinberg, Michele
  Steinberg*
Economics: *John Hoefle, Marcia Merry Baker,
  Paul Gallagher*
History: *Anton Chaitkin*
Ibero-America: *Dennis Small*
Russia and Eastern Europe: *Rachel Douglas*
United States: *Debra Freeman*

INTERNATIONAL BUREAUS
Bogotá: *Miriam Redondo*
Berlin: *Rainer Apel*
Copenhagen: *Tom Gillesberg*
Houston: *Harley Schlanger*
Lima: *Sara Madueño*
Melbourne: *Robert Barwick*
Mexico City: *Gerardo Castilleja Chávez*
New Delhi: *Ramtanu Maitra*
Paris: *Christine Bierre*
Stockholm: *Ulf Sandmark*
United Nations, N.Y.C.: *Leni Rubinstein*
Washington, D.C.: *William Jones*
Wiesbaden: *Göran Haglund*

ON THE WEB
e-mail: eirns@larouchepub.com
www.larouchepub.com
www.executiveintelligencereview.com
www.larouchepub.com/eiw
Webmaster: *John Sigerson*
Assistant Webmaster: *George Hollis*
Editor, Arabic-language edition: *Hussein Askary*

---

EIR (ISSN 0273-6314) *is published weekly
(50 issues), by EIR News Service, Inc.,
P.O. Box 17390, Washington, D.C. 20041-0390.
(703) 777-9451 ext. 415*

**European Headquarters:** E.I.R. GmbH, Postfach
Bahnstrasse 9a, D-65205, Wiesbaden, Germany
Tel: 49-611-73650
Homepage: http://www.eirna.com
e-mail: eirna@eirna.com
Director: Georg Neudecker

**Montreal, Canada:** 514-461-1557

**Denmark:** EIR - Danmark, Sankt Knuds Vej 11,
basement left, DK-1903 Frederiksberg, Denmark.
Tel.: +45 35 43 60 40, Fax: +45 35 43 87 57. e-mail:
eirdk@hotmail.com.

**Mexico City:** EIR, Sor Juana Inés de la Cruz 242-2
Col. Agricultura C.P. 11360
Delegación M. Hidalgo, México D.F.
Tel. (5525) 5318-2301
eirmexico@gmail.com

Canada Post Publication Sales Agreement
#40683579

**Postmaster:** Send all address changes to *EIR*, P.O.
Box 17390, Washington, D.C. 20041-0390.

Signed articles in *EIR* represent the views of the
authors, and not necessarily those of the Editorial
Board.

# Bring the U.S.
# Into the New Paradigm

# EIRContents

www.larouchepub.com Volume 43, Number 50, December 9, 2016

**Cover
This Week**

*The flags of the
United States,
China, and
Russia*

**BRINGING THE U.S. INTO
THE NEW PARADIGM**

## I. NEW POTENTIALS

**3 Grasping the Present Opportunity**
  by Robert Ingraham

**7 New Paradigm of the Belt and Road
Presented at Washington Seminar**
  by William Jones

**13** THE WHITE PAPER
  **China: Development Is an Inalienable Right**
  by William Jones

**16** INTERVIEW: Virginia State Senator Richard Black
  **A Time of Tremendous Hope**

## II. THE REAL ALEXANDER HAMILTON

**24 Hamilton's Controversial
Ally Dunlap: Opponent of
Slavery, Defender of
Progress**
  by Renée Sigerson

**27 Alexander Hamilton: To
Stimulate 'the Best Minds
and the Best Spirits'**

## III. THE FUTURE OF MANKIND

**28** RUSSIA AND CHINA RELY ON
CREATIVITY
  **Can Zero Be a Negative
Quantity? Yes, If It Is a
Zero-Deficit Budget!**
  by Helga Zepp-LaRouche

**31 Italy: The Third Shock**
  by Claudio Celani

# I. New Potentials

# Grasping the Present Opportunity

by Robert Ingraham

Dec. 4—In the 26 days since the U.S. Presidential election, the American people have been subjected to a roller-coaster array of conflicting emotions: hope, fear, uncertainty, triumphalism, despair—and just plain ordinary confusion. The shocking election results have left millions wondering exactly what to expect from the new administration.

Some individuals point, with hope, to President-Elect Trump's discussion of building infrastructure, re-enacting Glass-Steagall, and repairing relations with Russia. Others single out some of the recently announced Cabinet appointments, as well as both Mr. Trump's ties to Wall Street and his alleged bellicose stance on trade with China, as causes for deep concern. There is a great deal of speculation, both positive and negative, as to what to expect. But that is all that it is—speculation, the type that is fodder for internet blogs and gossip columnists. No one knows, as of this moment, exactly what the new President will do on Day 1 of his administration.

*en.kremlin.ru*

*Chinese President Xi Jinping and Russian President Vladimir Putin are offering the incoming Trump Presidency a new basis for relations.*

What the majority of observers fail to grasp, amidst all the confusion and misrepresentations, is the reality that, as of November 8, new and profound potentials have emerged as a strategic reality, potentials which may change the destiny of all mankind. Following the 1863 military victories of Vicksburg and Gettysburg, the entire nature of the American Civil War changed. The war was not won—and the ensuing months were fraught with dangers and struggle—but the conditions of the strategic battlefield were radically altered. That is where we find ourselves now.

The election results in the United States, and the impending regime change in Washington D.C., come at a moment when the world is being transformed by the actions of Russia and China. Since the Russian victory in 2009 in the Second Chechen War, and the 2012 ascension to power of Xi Jinping in China, Russia and China have together taken actions—through the BRICS, the Belt and Road Initiative (BRI), the Eurasian Economic Union, the Shanghai Cooperation Organization—as well as through many other institutions and initiatives—which have fundamentally changed the world. The old British Empire methods of colonialism and geopolitics are being replaced by a paradigm of friendship, cooperation and economic development.

Future progress, future development, future opportunities, future discoveries are now the governing philosophy within this new paradigm. This represents a radical altering of human relations on the planet, and the promise of even greater changes to come. It is within the context of these global shifts that the significance of what has occurred within the United States, as a result of the political revolution which took place on November 8, is to be located.

## I. A U.S./Russian Rapprochement

On November 30, 2016, Russian President Vladimir Putin delivered a speech to the Primakov Readings International Forum in Moscow. This was followed the very next day, December 1, by his Annual Presidential Address to the Federal Assembly, also in Moscow. The two speeches had different purposes, the first being given in honor of the recently deceased Yevgeny Primakov, the former Russian Prime Minister, and the December 1 "State of the Union" address primarily devoted to an official review of the Russian economy, social issues, and domestic policy.

In both of these speeches, President Putin offered an olive branch to the new Trump Administration, while at the same time making it clear that any improvement in relations will hinge on a clean break with the anti-Russian policies of George W. Bush and especially Barack Obama. On December 1, Putin stated,

"Russia is ready to work with the new U.S. Administration. It is important to put bilateral relations back on track and to develop them on an equal and mutually beneficial basis ... Cooperation between Russia and the United States in addressing global and regional issues will benefit the whole world. We have a shared responsibility to ensure international security and stability ...

"I certainly count on joining efforts with the United States in the fight against real rather than fictional threats, international terrorism being one of them ... We do not want confrontation with anyone. We have no need for it ... We do not seek and never have sought enemies. We need friends. But we will not allow our interests to be infringed upon or ignored."

In his remarks at the Primakov Forum, Putin pointed to Primakov's belief that "without a serious partnership between Russia and the United States," it would be difficult to address the world's "big challenges." With a new President soon to occupy the White House, Putin said, "We hope that this will create an opportunity to improve these relations, which are so important not only for our two peoples, but also for ensuring international stability and security," and he noted that in his recent phone conversations with President-elect Trump, the two agreed that "something must certainly be done about the current unsatisfactory state of bilateral relations."

Putin also pointed to Primakov's warnings against a policy of "regime-change," and even prior to the "Arab Spring," he said, Primakov had warned "about the disaster that would ensue" if secular Middle Eastern regimes were toppled. Here, again, the stated intentions of President-Elect Trump cohere with Russia's concerns and portend a dramatic shift in U.S. policy.

### Vladimir Putin: 'Our schools must promote creativity'

The general tenor of the bulk of President Putin's speech to the Federal Assembly could be described as "somber but optimistic," and determined to make further progress.

At the same time however, Putin identified the cultural and psychological upward shift which has become manifest within the Russian population, as it has fought against great odds and through great obstacles, to rebuild from the disaster of the late Soviet era and the post-Soviet catastrophes of the 1990s:

"Our people have united around patriotic values. We see this unity and we should thank them for it. They have united around these values not because everyone is happy and they have no demands; on the contrary, there is no shortage of problems and difficulties. But people have an understanding of their causes and, most importantly, are confident that together we can overcome these problems. It is this readiness to work for our country's sake and this sincere and deep-seated concern for Russia that form the foundation of this unity we see ... Let's remember that we are a single people, a united people, and we have only one Russia.

"Colleagues, the basis of our entire policy is to take care of people and increase human capital as Russia's most important resource. Therefore, our efforts are aimed at supporting the traditional values and the family, at [implementing] demographic programs, improving the environment and people's health, and promoting education and culture."

And, continuing into the area of youth and Russia's future, he said,

"Our schools must promote creativity. The children must learn to think independently, work both on their own and as part of a team, address unusual tasks and formulate and achieve goals, which will help them have an interesting and prosperous life ... We must promote the culture of research and engineering work. The number of cutting-edge science parks for children will increase to 40 within two years. They will serve as the basis for the development of a network of technical project groups across the country. Companies, universities, and research institutes should contribute to this, so that our children will see clearly that all of them have equal opportunities and an equal start in life, that Russia needs their ideas and knowledge and that they can prove their mettle in Russian companies and laboratories ...

"There are several things I would like to stress. Our education system must be based on the principle that all children and teenagers are gifted and can succeed in science, in creative areas and sport, in careers, and in life. Our task is to help them develop their talents. When they are successful, Russia is successful too. Colleagues, I view the young generation as Russia's reliable foundation in a turbulent and complicated 21st century. I believe that they are able not just to rise to challenges, but also to make their contribution to the development of the intellectual, technological and cultural agenda of global development."

As will become clear in the excerpts which will be given later in this article from Donald Trump's speech in Cincinnati, Ohio, there is a common theme—a human theme—that is interwoven throughout both that speech as well as the above cited remarks from Vladimir Putin. To wit: the improvement of life for the common citizen; peace and cooperation among nations; the fostering of industry, science, and education; and a commitment to the development of the potentials of youth for the creation of a better future.

There is much that can be built upon there.

c-span

*President-elect Trump, speaking in Cincinnati, Ohio on December 1.*

## II. China: an 'Inalienable Right to Development'

Within this issue of *EIR* there are to be found two articles by William Jones. The first deals with a major White Paper released by the Chinese government, titled, "The Right to Development: China's Philosophy, Practice, and Contribution"; the second reports on *EIR*'s participation in a November 30, Washington, D.C. event on the Belt and Road Initiative (BRI), sponsored by the China Energy Fund Committee and the Asia Society.

Readers of this article must study those two pieces by William Jones, for once again, they define, together with the offerings of friendship and cooperation by Vladimir Putin, a decisive opportunity for the incoming Trump Administration to shatter and expunge all of the geopolitical nightmares of the Bush/Obama years.

Simply put, the Chinese White Paper states,

"The right to development must be enjoyed and shared by all peoples. Realizing the right to development is the responsibility of all countries and also the obligation of the international community. It requires governments of all countries to formulate development strategies and policies suited to their own realities, and it requires concerted efforts of the international community as a whole."

The November 30 event, attended by *EIR*, could be characterized as the opening salvo of the New Paradigm knocking on the door of Washington, D.C. As reported by Jones, most of the American participants had great difficulty in breaking with the mentality of geopolitics and imperial confrontation, but one after aother

of the Chinese speakers laid out the great projects being built, and the great opportunities for both the United States and the rest of the world. Dr. Patrick Ho, the Secretary General of the China Energy Fund Committee, concluded the event with the admonition, "It's not possible for one section of the world to alone have a sense of prosperity. The Belt and Road is not a sphere of influence, but an accommodating of different interests, a vision that keeps on unfolding."

Thus, as in the case of Vladimir Putin, China is offering the incoming Trump Presidency a new basis for relations and a new path for the human race.

## III. Donald Trump in Cincinnati

What is presented here are verbatim excerpts from the speech which President-Elect Trump delivered in Cincinnati, Ohio on December 1. There were other things also said in that speech which *EIR* and Lyndon LaRouche might not agree with, and there were certain aspects which may prove problematic in the months to come. But, within the context of what was presented above concerning the initiatives being taken by China and Russia, these remarks are a breath of fresh air for America and the trans-Atlantic world. Ask yourself this question: When was the last time you heard an American leader speak like this? Even remotely?

Trump said: "One of the reasons we are so divided today is because the government has failed to protect the interests of the American workers and their families, making it too easy to see ourselves as distinct groups and not unified as a whole ... Washington's politicians have spent so long appealing to competing interests, they've forgotten how to appeal to the national interest, combining the skills and talents of our people in a common cause… But that is all about to change. Our goal is to strengthen the bonds of trust between citizens, to restore our sense of membership in a shared national community. We are going to seek a truly inclusive society where we support each other, love each other, and look out for each other.

"We're going to bring back the American Dream. The problems that plague American cities or that afflict poor rural communities—and we do have rural communities; some of them are poor—we're going to help these people; we're going to rebuild these communities. They're not permanent features of American life. They can be fixed, and, together, we are going to fix them.

"People are constantly telling me and telling you to reduce our expectations. Those people are fools. They are fools … Anything we want for our country is now possible. Anything. Now is not the time to downsize our dreams, but to set our sights higher than ever before for our country. Now is the time to push for real profound change that restores the full promise of America for all its people, and those people are great people … Now is the time to unlock the potential of millions of Americans left on the sidelines, their talents unused, their dreams unrealized and their aspirations totally forgotten. These are people of great talent. This is the moment. This is our chance. This is our window for action. This is the hour when the great deeds can be done, and our highest hopes come true. We're going to do it, folks; we're going to do it.

"We will build new roads, tunnels, bridges, railways, airports, schools, and hospitals, including major projects in the inner-cities. There's such potential in the inner-cities, we're not using our potential … We will deepen our harbors, we have harbors that ships can't even get into … We're going to fight for every last American job. It's time to remove the rust from the rust belt and usher in a new industrial revolution. We're going to do it.

"We will pursue a new foreign policy, one which finally learns from the mistakes of the past. We will stop trying to topple regimes and overthrowing governments … Our goal is stability, not chaos … We've spent $6 trillion in the Middle East, and the Middle East today is far worse than it's ever been. You will see changes very quickly.

"We are a nation that won two world wars, dug out the Panama Canal, put a man on the Moon and satellites all over outer space, but somewhere along the way we started thinking small. I'm asking you to dream big again, and bold and daring things for your country will happen once again. I'm asking you to join me in this next chapter of this unbelievable and unprecedented movement, as we work toward prosperity at home, peace abroad, and new frontiers in science, technology, and space. I'm asking you to believe in America again. We have many challenges, but this is truly an exciting time to be alive …. The script is not yet written. We do not know what the next page will read, but what we do know is that the pages will be authored by each one of you. Each one of you. Americans will be the captains of their own destiny once again. I talked about our great movement, but you are the movement; I'm just the messenger."

# IV. Our approach

There are many danger signs ahead, both from within the United States, but more ominously, emanating from the extended power structures of the British financial empire, as well as the current pre-war deployment of NATO. They have suffered a defeat, but they are not defeated.

Adding to the difficulties is the unpleasant reality that the intellectual competence of American leaders has declined precipitously since the death of Franklin Roosevelt in 1945. Today, with this great opportunity before us, will those leaders—or the American people—look a gift horse in the mouth? Will they fail to act on what is being offered? Will they understand what is at stake? For too many, in Congress and elsewhere, the answers to those questions are Yes, Yes, and No.

Our approach is simple. We must act—and demand that others, of whatever political stripe or background, also act—on the principles embodied in Lyndon LaRouche's "Four Laws to Save the U.S.A." Those principles are not only coherent with the intentions declaimed by Vladimir Putin and Xi Jinping; they go to an even higher level in defining the human mission.

As stated, the Trump victory of November 8 has transformed the battlefield. We must think and act accordingly.

Our goal is to bring the United States into the New Global Paradigm. That is the Prize. Don't take your eyes off it. Do not be distracted by secondary issues. Disagreements on non-essential "programmatic" points or setbacks on issues of lesser importance must be ignored. Bring the United States into a full partnership with the nations of China and Russia. That will win everything.

# New Paradigm of the Belt and Road Presented at Washington Seminar

by William Jones

Dec. 2—China's Belt and Road Initiative has been garnering a great deal of interest in think-tanks around Washington in the aftermath of the U.S. elections, where some shift in U.S. foreign policy is expected as the new Trump Administration takes form. An event on November 30 organized by the China Energy Fund Committee and the Institute for the Analysis of Global Security (IAGS) was something of a watershed in presenting the full breadth of the Belt and Road policy and tracking the reaction from the American side. While the forum gave an opportunity to both a high-level Chinese delegation and a group of U.S. think-tankers to present their views on the Belt and Road, in an attempt to find some level of agreement on U.S.-China cooperation with the Belt and Road, the forum also revealed stark differences in the philosophical outlooks from which the project is viewed from the two sides.

EIRNS/Jason Ross

*Professor Liu Weidong in an exchange from the conference floor.*

The wide-ranging initiative put forward by President Xi Jinping in September 2013 was initially called "*One* Belt, *One* Road." The name is now deemed out-of-date, given that there are now *six* different routes of the Belt and Road, and it has been appropriately rechristened as simply the Belt and Road Initiative (BRI).

While the initiative is based on the construction of major transportation grids, including high-speed rail, conventional rail, highways, and seaports, these simply provide the basic platform for major investment and overall development in the regions crisscrossed by the transportation grid. It is a project that far outstrips the post-World War II Marshall Plan in scale, but its proponents shy away from comparisons with the Cold War Marshall Plan because it represents a new paradigm of thought. It rather harks back to the days of cooperation, trade, and cultural interpenetration which existed during the period of the ancient Silk Road.

The cultural paradigm shift represented by the BRI was most beautifully elaborated at the beginning and end of the forum by Patrick Ho, the secretary general of the China Energy Fund Committee, who had taken the initiative to organize the forum. "We live today in a threatened world," he said. "There is great poverty, and

EIRNS/Jason Ross
*Chen Guoqiang*

EIRNS/Jason Ross
*Zhao Jinping*

China "had reached a new bottleneck in development and sought a "new model of growth and development." "It found this in peaceful co-development and sharing with its neighbors, with a program which now encompasses 60 countries, affecting 4.9 billion people," he said. As became clear during the course of the day, the issue of "inclusiveness" was something of a stumbling bloc for some of the U.S. interlocutors.

Chen Guoqiang, Director General in the Department of International Cooperation at the Development Research Center (DRC) of the State Council of China, lamented the lack of understanding in the West of the Belt and Road Initiative. He attributed this to the lack of information people are getting here and to consideration of what some people feel are their vested interests. He also expressed concern that too few Chinese scholars have come to the United States to explain the goals and the purpose of the initiative. Chen pointed out that under the present economic order, developing countries—totally dependent on developed countries—have not received the benefits of globalization.

although we have enough sources to go around for all of us, 2.8 billion people still lack resources. There is a lack of clean water for billions of people. Globalization created development as well as new problems. We are not sharing the fruits of progress."

## Inclusiveness a Stumbling Block

"Globalization is now a system in crisis, a broken system. It cannot advance human progress. There are too many people left behind. We now need a holistic model that will be all-inclusive and a shift to a more sustainable and useful model," Ho said. The Belt and Road is the form of that model. "Inclusiveness and sharing is the basis of the Belt and Road." For China, he said, this was of great importance. Now having become the second largest economy in the world,

## Case for the Belt and Road

The purpose of the BRI is to create an economic order based on sharing, he said. The BRI is also consistent with China's own domestic development program, China 2030. "Both programs respect the development priorities of each country and both stress the need for infrastructure," Chen said. "The expansion of the BRI will provide benefits to China as well as to the world."

"First," Chen said, "it will provide sustainable public goods; second, it will further the extension of China's development experience and its successful poverty reduction; and third, it will feature South-South cooperation as well as tripartite cooperation.

Zhao Jinping, also with the State Council's DRC, underlined that the BRI would create a new space of cooperation and that it would also include the United States and Japan. It was also necessary, Zhao underlined, to enhance North-South and East-West cooperation. Liu Weidong called the Belt and Road a new stage of "inclusive globalization," quoting a Chinese proverb, "In order to become rich, build a road." Professor Li Xiangyang noted that the principle of "righteousness before profit was also relevant to the BRI. "President Xi said that we should have profit but also increase respect for China in the world. For the Belt and Road Initiative there is no set timetable and there are no quantitative measures," Zhao said.

During the lunch session, Ziad Haider, the Special Representative for Commercial and Business Affairs at the U.S. Department of State, spoke of the U.S. view of the BRI. While the Obama Administration has largely ignored the BRI and discouraged other countries from joining the China-promoted Asian Infrastructure Investment Bank (AIIB), Haider indicated that there was some cooperation on the diplomatic level. He began his talk by focussing on the tremendous infrastructure needs of the world.

Haider called the BRI an "integrated vision" and indicated that there was an interest at the State Department in getting U.S. firms involved. He noted the Belt and Road's importance in investment in infrastructure, in customs harmonization, and in the innovation connections in the Belt and Road countries. He said there were possibilities for more funding from the Overseas Private Investment Corp. (OPIC) and involvement of the Export-Import Bank to help U.S. firms participate. "China shouldn't be the only player in this space," Haider said. He also said that the State Department is working together with China's National Development

EIRNS/Jason Ross
*Gal Luft*

EIRNS/Jason Ross
*Christina Lin*

and Reform Commission, the agency primarily tasked with the development of the BRI. He also indicated that there was some progress toward cooperating with the AIIB.

## Ingrained Geopolitics

While in the morning, there had been a session on the infrastructure needs of the world, focussing on the economic aspects of the Belt and Road, in the afternoon session, a number of scholars from Washington think-tanks dealt with some of the political aspects.

The aspects and concerns that they brought up clearly indicated the problems the U.S. side has in understanding the underlying philosophy of the Belt and Road. It was already manifest during part of the luncheon discussion, when Gal Luft from the IAGS re-

EIRNS/Jason Ross
*Richard Hoagland*

EIRNS/Jason Ross
*Daniel Markey*

EIRNS/Jason Ross
*Bill Jones*

viewed a report he had done on the topic—made available at the event—entitled, "It Takes a Road: China's Belt and Road Initiative: An American Response." While the report had some very interesting details and maps of the Belt and Road routes, Luft's comments were entirely imbued with geopolitical restrictions and considerations, reflecting the predominantly geopolitical outlook of the U.S. establishment that would quickly turn the BRI into a distant pipe-dream. Luft indicated great concern, for instance, over the railroad through Iran, since he didn't think it would be proper to make Iran a "gate-keeper" of the Belt and Road.

This was also apparent in the afternoon panel with

the U.S. think-tanks. While some of speakers, such as Christina Lin from the Center for Transatlantic Relations at Johns Hopkins, tried to get her fellow panelists to understand that we are now moving toward a "multipolar world," most of the others were not at all keen on accepting that idea. Richard Hoagland, a former U.S. Ambassador to Kazakstan, who had expressed interest in the Belt and Road when President Xi announced the project, commented, rather cryptically, that in these big projects there are always "winners and losers." But of course, in the geopolitical world, there is only a zero-sum game! Most telling were the comments of Daniel Markey, a senior research professor at the Johns Hopkins School of Advanced International Studies.

## Geopolitics Confronted

Earlier in the day, *EIR*'s Bill Jones had raised the problem of the "geopolitical outlook prevailing in Gal Luft's presentation," noting that "the BRI could only succeed if we abandoned the geopolitical" mindset. Markey, perhaps referring to that little encounter, here rushed to the defense of geopolitics. Markey has made his professional mark in dealing with Pakistan, and was highly critical of China's plan to build a road from Kashgar in western China to the port of Gwadar in Pakistan. Given the extreme poverty in the region and the unstable political situation, he thought that China's only reason for building a road in this devastated region was geopolitical, namely for China to gain access to the Indian Ocean, making a rather snide comment that geopolitics cannot be replaced by "geo-economics."

In the following Q&A, Jones directed a question to Markey, commenting sarcastically, "Oh, of course, such devastated areas like Syria or Iraq, or Gaza or even the Bronx, for that matter, would not be the most appropriate place to launch a Silk Road project. But the fact of the matter is that if you *don't* launch a Silk Road there, they will always remain hellholes for the people living there!" Even some of the panel nodded in agreement with Jones' comment. While Markey fended this off somewhat cavalierly, he then

THE THREE "KNOCKS" – THE WORLD TRYING TO UNDERSTAND CHINA

1st Knock
Priests and Sinologists
1583

2nd Knock
Arms and Troops
1840

3rd Knock
Market Economy and International Trade
1972

*Jesuit missionary Matteo Ricci (left) and a collaborator, the scholar Xu Guangqi (right), who took the name Paul, in a 1667 book illustration.*

got hit with a question from Alicia Cerretani with LaRouche PAC, who asked why Markey thought there was such a disconnect between the Chinese view and the American view he was expressing. Caught a bit off-guard by this, he wheedled his way out of that one too.

But this back-and-forth on the issue of geopolitics brought some of the Chinese speakers to their feet. Professor Liu Weidong expressed his frustration with the Americans who always try to "politicize" these issues that deal with the fate of millions of people. "That's not the way we think about these things," he said. Professor Zhao Jinping also expressed his objections. "With China's rise, the United States always says it wants China to play a greater role. But China has fulfilled its responsibility as a major power by developing the Belt and Road. But some countries don't see the BRI in a positive light. You have to understand that many countries have a terrible development gap. We don't like everyone looking at this through a political lens. We certainly don't, and this is a consensus we have come to in our study of the Belt and Road."

## The Stretto

Toward the conclusion of the forum, Patrick Ho had prepared his stretto to this somewhat dissonant symphony which he had helped to organize, presenting an expansive view of the development of China, leading to this present development in world history. "It is not possible for one section alone to have a sense of prosperity," he said. "What we need today is a strategy for development, a long-lasting and sustainable one. We need wise consultation and joint contribution. Only through a win-win strategy can we gain a foothold. The Belt and Road is not a sphere of influence, but an accommodating of interests. It paves the way for the common destiny of mankind."

Ho then went through the need to create a broad understanding of this project in order for it to succeed. Noting the rise of China in the period of its greatness, he also noted the "disconnect" in the understanding of China. "It may take hundreds of years for the West to understand China," he said. "Marco Polo began the quest and then it was continued by the Jesuits Matteo Ricci and Joachim Bouvet [a correspondent of Leibniz]. This was the first dialogue between the two giant civilizations. And then the doors were callously closed."

"After this, the Western countries expanded colonialism to the East," Ho said, beginning what for China were a hundred years of humiliation. Now with the Belt and Road, China has re-emerged from those depths and become a major player. "The Belt and Road is a vision rather than a project, and a vision which is constantly expanding and may always do so. It is a connection of hearts and minds connecting souls, connecting the Chinese Dream with the American Dream and other dreams, freedom from want, freedom from fear, harmony with nature, and peace."

*Patrick Ho*

EIRNS/Jason Ross

He encouraged the United States to take part in this vision, proposing that the new Trump Administration consider the BRI as a platform for closer cooperation between the United States and China, realigning trade to accommodate the BRI, adjusting its posture in the international development banks to support infrastructure, and helping with security along the Belt and Road.

It is certainly to be hoped that the Trump Administration will agree to these proposals, but as we can see from the day's forum, it will take an effort to change the mindset of our elected leaders who have such difficulty with that "vision thing." We must begin by explaining to the American people, who have been so disappointed recently by the quality of political leadership in Washington, that there is a vision of a better world in which they also can be a part. They simply have to raise their eyes above the immediate horizon to see it, and to act accordingly to bring sanity to our nation's institutions.

# THE WHITE PAPER

# China: Development Is an Inalienable Right

by William Jones

Dec. 3—On the occasion of the 30th anniversary of the UN Declaration on the Right to Development, China's State Council Information Office on Dec. 1 issued a white paper on the right to development,[1] detailing the country's philosophy, practice, and contribution with respect to this principle.

While the world has already been astonished by China's success in raising 700 million people out of poverty, the white paper presents extraordinary details of its development over the last three decades, and firmly asserts that this is not something that can be peculiar to China, but must become a paradigm for the entire world.

The white paper begins with a clear statement: "Development is a universal human theme, providing for people's basic needs and giving them hope of a better life. The right to development is an inalienable human right, symbolizing dignity and honor. Only through development can we address global challenges; only through development can we protect basic civil rights of the people; only through development can we promote the progress of human society."

The report refers to the oft-forgotten history of China before the "hundred years of humiliation" when

wikipedia/Alex Needham
*Complex traffic exchange in Puxi, the historic center of Shanghai.*

China lived under the colonialist boot. "In ancient times, China was for long the world leader in agriculture, and contributed to human progress with extraordinary development achievements," the report states. "Studies reveal that until the mid-19th century, China's GDP and per capita GDP were the world's highest. Before the 16th century, China contributed 173 of the world's top 300 innovations and discoveries."

And then came the age when the imperial powers ran roughshod over China. "Repeated invasions by foreign powers, particularly from the West, from 1840 to 1949, and China's corrupt ruling class and backward social system reduced China to a semi-colonial and semi-feudal society. There was constant warfare, an unstable society, economic depression, no security of livelihood, and extreme poverty."

---

1. "The Right to Development: China's Philosophy, Practice and Contribution," issued by the State Council Information Office of the People's Republic of China, December 1, 2016. The full text: http://news. xinhuanet.com/english/china/2016-12/01/c_135873721.htm

## Rising Living Standards

With the establishment of the People's Republic in 1949, China started on the road to assuming its rightful place as a major power on the world stage. During the current period of "reform and opening up," China has lifted 700 million people out of poverty, a figure that accounts for more than 70% of the global reduction in poverty. The number of people still living in poverty in China represents 5.7% of the total population, making China the first nation to reach the UN Millennium Development Goals in poverty reduction. In March 2016, China announced that it intends to eliminate poverty entirely among the rural poor by 2020.

The report notes that China feeds more than 20% of the world's population with less than 10% of the world's arable land. It has established the largest social security system in the world, and average life expectancy had grown from 35 years of age in 1949 to 76.3 years in 2015. China has instituted a unified, basic old-age insurance system for urban and rural residents throughout the country. By the end of 2015, China had established a medical insurance system covering nearly all its citizens. The basic medical insurance for urban workers and residents, and the new rural cooperative medical insurance, cover 1.3 billion people, keeping the percentage of those insured above 95%.

Living standards have significantly improved. From 1978 to 2015, the annual gross domestic product (GDP) increased from 368 billion RMB[2] to 68,550 billion RMB, and per capita GDP increased from $200 in 1978 to $8,000 in 2015. The Engel coefficient, the percentage of household income spent on food, in 1978 was 57% for urban households and 68% for rural households. In 2015 those figures were 30% and 33%, respectively.

From 2011 to 2015, more than 5.5 million unemployed urban people found jobs every year, while an annual average of almost 1.8 million people who had difficulty in securing jobs, found employment. While the downturn in the export market has had its discernible effect on employment, the Chinese government is now working to have many migrant workers go back to their home towns to set up local businesses. The expansion of the Internet to rural areas has increased the ability of rural households to reach out to more distant consumers.

Thomas Galvez

*Baibi Mountain Village School in Guizhou Province, China.*

## Rising Literacy and Culture

China has instituted a system of compulsory education. In 1949, 80% of the national population was illiterate, and the enrollment rate of school children was only 20%. In 2015, the net enrollment rate of primary school-age children was 99.8%; in nine-year compulsory education, 93%; in high school, 87%. The enrollment rate for higher education has reached a level approaching that of medium-developed countries.

In the area of culture more broadly, the Chinese government has sought to raise the intellectual level of the general population. By the end of 2015, China had 2,037 art troupes, 3,139 public libraries, 3,315 cultural centers, 2,981 museums, 40 provincial digital libraries, and 479 municipal and prefectural digital libraries.

In 2015, China printed more than 43 billion copies of newspapers, 2.9 billion copies of periodicals, and 8.7 billion copies of books. At the end of the 2015, radio coverage reached 98.2%, and television coverage 98.8% of the total population. (This television is not the mind-rot we see in the United States today.) In 2015, China produced 395 TV serials totaling 16,560 episodes, 134,000 minutes of television animation, 686 feature films, and 202 popular science films, documentaries, animation, and special films. China has launched a nationwide "All People Reading" campaign. A 2016 "Literary China" series of activities has benefitted more than 800 million participants, forming a congenial social atmosphere for reading.

---

2. The current exchange rate is 7 RMB to the dollar.

A great deal of effort has also been spent in promoting the many minority cultures in China. This includes preserving works of literature in the minority languages and publishing them for broader circulation. In 2015 China produced 69 million copies of 9,192 book titles, 196 million copies of newspapers, and 12.4 million copies of periodicals in ethnic minority languages. Nearly 200 radio stations nationwide broadcast in 25 ethnic minority languages and 37 ethnic minority dialects.

## Unprecedented Outreach

The success of China's development has become a major part of the country's "going out" policy. The Belt and Road Initiative and collaborative programs and institutions have promoted the development of the neighboring countries. Over the past 60 years, China has provided approximately 400 billion RMB in aid to 166 countries and international organizations. It has trained more than 12 million personnel from developing countries and dispatched more than 600,000 people to aid development abroad.

In the coming five years, China will implement six "One Hundred Programs" targeting developing countries, namely, 100 poverty reduction programs, 100 for agricultural cooperation, 100 for trade aid, 100 for environmental protection, 100 hospitals and clinics, and 100 schools and vocational training centers. Training opportunities (120,000) and scholarships (150,000) will be made available to developing countries in China, and 500,000 vocational technical personnel will be trained. China will also set up a South-South Cooperation and Development Academy.

The scope of this vast development program—what China has accomplished and what it now envisions—is unlike anything the world has ever seen. But U.S. politicians still look askance at China's achievements and eye with suspicion China's successful efforts to help other nations lift themselves up. While the United States has prided itself as being that "city on the hill" that assists other nations to develop, the most recent decades have seen little but death and devastation wreaked on impoverished nations by the militarily most powerful nation in the world. Now that a newly revived China is standing up to carry its own weight in healing the world's wounds, it behooves our nation's leaders to join in that effort—or at least to applaud China's efforts in doing so—instead of grousing in the corner like a frightened child, plotting devious ways to reassert American "hegemony."

# Syria: A Time of Tremendous Hope

*The following interview with Virginia State Senator Richard Black was conducted Dec. 1 by* EIR *Editor William Wertz.*

My name is Will Wertz. I'm a member of the editorial board of *Executive Intelligence Review,* and we are here today interviewing Richard Black, who has really stood up in a unique and courageous way over really a long period in fighting for principle, in a number of nations across the globe, certainly including the United States, but, especially in the Middle East and northern Africa, opposing the policy of regime change which has targeted many countries which, ironically, are countries where there has been religious freedom, where you have secular governments, where people have lived together from different ethnic backgrounds and religious denominations for centuries. And we are meeting today because the battle of Aleppo is in the process of being resolved.

As you may have seen in the news, in recent days the Syrian Army and its allies, with the support of the Russians, have liberated over 40% of eastern Aleppo. That is, something in the range of 90,000 people were liberated, many of those, children. Tens of thousands of people who had been held hostage by the terrorists, by Al-Qaeda, which is the actual way to identify Al-Nusra, and all of the "moderate" terrorists who work with Al-Qaeda/Al-Nusra, have now been able to leave the city. There are reports of tens of thousands of people who are now fleeing out of the humanitarian corridors which the Syrians had set up, but which the terrorists had mined and had shelled in order to prevent them from leaving. Many of these are children; there are many who require medical treatment. The Russians are sending in mobile hospitals to help out in the situation.

It is a little bit over a year ago, in September of last year, that President Putin of Russia went before the General Assembly at the UN and proposed an international coalition to fight terrorism, similar to the international coalition which succeeded in defeating the Nazis over 70 years before. Unfortunately, under the Obama administration, that proposal for an international coalition was not acted upon. Today, in Russia, Putin reiterated that call. He signed a decree which is entitled, "The New Foreign Policy Concept of Russia," in which he called for a broad international anti-terrorism coalition which would be based upon respect for international law, respect for the diversity of people throughout the world. And we have a situation in the world, following the recent election in the United States, where perhaps it will be possible for the United States to change direction in a decisive way, and join in such an effort which would be to the benefit of all humanity.

So I wanted to just start out with your assessment of the situation surrounding the battle of Aleppo, and also what the prospects are for changing the course of U.S. policy.

**Sen. Richard Black:** Well, first of all, going back a number of months, the Syrian Army has managed, through some very fine tactical maneuvers, managed to cut off and isolate the Aleppo pocket. The Aleppo pocket is said to contain 275,000 civilians. This is the official UN and mainstream media figure. I question it; my guess is that the actual number is perhaps significantly less than this. However, what happened within the last week is that, in the northern part of this, roughly a kidney-shaped pocket, there was a tremendous moral and military collapse of Al-Qaeda, and its allies, and they essentially panicked, they went into a full-bore retreat. The Syrian Army moved very quickly and took over almost half of the entire Aleppo pocket.

In the course of this, we had been told by the media that somehow President Assad was surrounding the Aleppo pocket with desires of killing everybody who was inside. Well, he had set up a number of humanitarian corridors; he had tried to get the terrorists to allow the escape of the civilians so that they wouldn't be caught in the middle. When the first civilians tried to get out, I'm not sure how many actually tried to move through one of the corridors, 26 of them were machine gunned and killed. There have been other attempts and, at first, the Al-Qaeda and their allies were able, through snipers and so forth, were able to kill all of the people trying to escape, or almost all.

With the cataclysmic collapse of the northern end of the Aleppo pocket, they simply could not maintain control. They were so busy trying to stay alive, they were just trying to get out of there; there was a massive flood of refugees. At first they reported 600, then 1,500, then it went up, and before long it was 10,000, then 15,000. I've even seen a figure of 30,000. I don't know whether that is accurate. But there are certainly photos and videos of massive numbers, crowds of people, and the Syrian government—they are not killing them as they were supposed to be doing according to the mainstream media—they are sending buses to pick them up; they are sending troops to do some very rudimentary screening to make sure people don't slip in wearing suicide bombs and kill a lot of civilians.

So, throughout the war, President Assad has consistently maintained this policy of allowing civilians to escape the battleground, and sometimes it's been frustrating to military people like myself. I fought in some of the most fierce combat with the First Marine Regiment, and to allow your enemy to escape, is frustrating, but what he [Assad] is doing is he's trying to, number one, save the lives of civilians; and number two, preserve infrastructure, because he knows that eventually he has to rebuild the country. And so he allows them to escape. We don't know exactly what will happen in Aleppo. The fighting continues, but it is clear that the terrorists are going to lose the battle for Aleppo, and the government is going to secure the Aleppo pocket.

Every time that they are on the losing end, the UN can be counted on to demand to have a stop, a ceasefire, a pause, so that additional weapons can be sent in to the terrorists. The time for this is finished. I don't think we will see another humanitarian pause. I think the battle will continue until it reaches its conclusion. And so I think we will see that the Aleppo pocket has essentially been a tumor, like a cancerous tumor of terrorists. Now

EIRNS/Stuart Lewis

*Virginia State Senator Richard Black*

remember, Al-Nusra is the group that holds together all of the others. Al-Nusra is Al-Qaeda in Syria. Al-Qaeda is the group that flew the planes into the Twin Towers and sent 3,000 Americans to their fiery deaths, a quarter of a mile below the top of the Twin Towers.

We should be rejoicing that we have captured Al-Qaeda's biggest army in Aleppo and that they are going to be destroyed. So, what will happen at this point? Aleppo will be completely liberated. Now, keep in mind that the Aleppo pocket has only been about one eighth of Aleppo. It's always described in the media as, well, Aleppo is roughly divided into half. It's not. It's clearly not. They've claimed a quarter of a million people, and at the same time all figures are that there are at least a million people in the government-held area of Aleppo. It's irrational to claim that they have held half of Aleppo; they haven't. They've held a small portion, and it's growing smaller. It may be a twelfth, a fifteenth, a sixteenth of Aleppo, but it is a small and shrinking tumorous mass that will eventually disappear, and hopefully the city will be cancer-free and there will be no more of Al-Qaeda.

## A Change in U.S. Policy

So, I think there is tremendous hope. The plan is to basically take this off the plate before the new Administration [in Washington] takes power, so that they don't even have to deal with it. They will certainly achieve that. I think there is no doubt that that will occur before January 20th. Where does that leave us? I think we have a new Administration coming in; [President-elect] Donald Trump, in my view, has expressed a very clear vision of what's going on in Syria. His National Security Adviser, Lt. General Michael Flynn, clearly understands the nature of the terrorists who have been invading Syria. He warned Obama repeatedly that the ratline which was the transfer of weapons from Libya into Turkey and across the border into Syria, originally it was purportedly designed to supply weapons to moderate rebels. The Defense Intelligence Agency, in 2013, rendered explicit findings in which they said this had degenerated into an indiscriminate program which supplied all rebels, and they explicitly named Al-Qaeda and ISIS.

The United States taxpayer was funding Al-Qaeda and ISIS, and so this will end. I have every reason to believe, I think that under Donald Trump, and with Lt. General Flynn, I think what we are likely to see is a total cutoff of weapons going to all of these traditional terrorists, and we may still see weapons reach the Kurds along the Turkish border, because Syria is facing a very dangerous invasion by Turkey and by President Erdogan, who has become an absolute dictator and tyrant. He has not only invaded Syria, but he's also invaded our ally Iraq. And so I think as far as the rest of the terrorists, the terrorists are quickly being purged from the whole Damascus area. That has been a stronghold of theirs throughout the war. Damascus is being taken. It will leave them with one area that they control in Idlib, but Idlib does not begin to compare to Damascus or to Aleppo.

And so I think we will see, I believe we'll see, a partnership between Russia and the United States in fighting genuine terrorism, not only in Syria, but I think throughout the world. And I think this is a very positive development. Under President Obama we've seen an explosion of terrorism across the globe. We've seen it hit cities across the United States. We had a Somali incident, a fellow—we keep bringing in people who come with a tremendous hatred of this country and a desire to commit acts of jihad, and just two days ago, we had one of those. They seem to happen almost weekly now.

I think Syria has been the breeding ground for terrorism. Saudi Arabia gives them this vile Wahhabi philosophy which teaches them that they are to go forth, they are to purge the world of Christians, Jews, Buddhists, Hindus, everybody except Wahhabis, including Sunni Muslims, if they do not adapt to seventh-century standards. So I think there is a great deal of reason to hope, and I think we are going to see very good things in the coming year.

### Turning Back Barbarism

**Wertz:** Now, you've been in Syria, including to Palmyra, I believe, and of course when the Syrian Army liberated Palmyra, there was no celebration among the supporters of the so-called moderate terrorists in Syria from the West.

**Black:** No!

**Wertz:** Similarly, as Aleppo has been in the process of being liberated, you've had calls from the U.S., from the United Kingdom, from France to impose sanctions on the Russians for the liberation of Aleppo from terrorists. You were mentioning the whole question of Al-Qaeda. The fact of the matter is that the head of Al-Qaeda, [Ayman] al-Zawahiri, about a year ago, called for Al-Nusra to create an Al-Qaeda Caliphate in Syria.

**Black:** Yes, there's no doubt. It started off where the two progeny of Al-Qaeda worldwide were ISIS and Al-Nusra. They began to squabble among themselves, to fight among themselves, but philosophically they are very much like two drug cartels. They have absolutely the same objective, which is to spread heroin, cocaine, all sorts of narcotics throughout the world, but they conflict because they each want leadership. There is no greater difference; ISIS and Al-Nusra are identical in terms of their philosophy. They believe that not only should they conquer Syria, but they believe that they should go forth, they should conquer Europe; I think Europe is clearly in their sights.

There is no question that if the Obama Administration had succeeded in toppling President Assad, we would have had an Al-Qaeda or Al-Nusra government and we would have gone into one of these seventh-century caliphates. We would have seen slave markets, just as we've seen in ISIS; we would have seen the beheading of millions of Christians, Alawites, Shiites, Druze. We would have seen their children and their wives sold as sex-slaves—because this is what they do. And we—fortunately—we have documentary proof of it, and I will tell you, I have watched one thousand videos, because I don't believe in getting information secondhand; and because they believe in terrorism, the terrorists love to put evidence of what they do on video. And so, I have watched one thousand people beheaded. I have watched thousands of people lined up and executed and fall into graves. I've watched people burn to death; I've watched people crucified. These are the people that we consider "moderate rebels." And these are the people we have supported.

When I went to Palmyra—which was just disgraceful that we had allowed it to fall—Palmyra was one of the gems of all human civilization; it contained four thousand years of layer after layer of temples and monuments and so forth. When Jesus walked the earth, Palmyra was two thousand years old, and the ISIS troops who seized it had to cross 100 miles of barren desert. There was no cover, there was no concealment, there were no dust storms because this is all rock, it's not

*Tetrapylon in Palmyra.*

creative commons

sand. And so the American-led coalition saw this massive army with hundreds of tanks and artillery pieces and armored vehicles and trucks and so forth, and watched them move across to Palmyra, where they proceeded to defeat the Syrian Army, seize the place, and they began blowing down ancient Roman columns that had stood for thousands of years perfectly preserved; and they destroyed them.

Why did we not drop a single bomb? And I have confirmed we did not drop a single bomb to stop this massive army that was in clear view. The reason is because from where ISIS stood, to where Palmyra stood, to where Damascus, the capitol of Syria stood, Palmyra was halfway. If they could seize Palmyra, the hope was of the American-led coalition, that they would forge on and they would seize Damascus. Had they seized Damascus, they would have purged it of all evidence of civilization just as they have attempted to do in Palmyra; and we have always rooted, we have always thrown our full diplomatic support towards those who behead priests, who rape nuns, who rape little girls. One of the leaders of one of these terrorist groups had a 13-year-old little girl whom he gang-raped, and when he would ride into battle, in his American built armored Humvee, he would strap her to the windshield, because he knew that the Syrian soldiers were civilized and they would not kill a young naked helpless girl. And that was his defense.

The war crimes on the side of the people that we have supported have been grotesque. They have equaled or exceeded anything that ever happened with the Nazis in the Second World War, and yet we have funded them, we have armed them; we have given them our full diplomatic support. I think it's one of the great stains on the history of America, and one that I hope that the new Administration will reverse.

## Binding up the Nation's Wounds

**Wertz:** One of the things that is generally not known is that Assad has essentially offered a pardon to any militant who lays down his arms and is willing to settle his legal status. This included, just in the recent days, over 500 armed men who left eastern Aleppo, and 484 of those were immediately pardoned by the Assad government because they were local residents of Aleppo.

**Black:** They are taken under the wings of the Reconciliation Commission, and they are questioned to be sure that there are not some who are extreme war criminals. Many of those freed are going to be war criminals, but unless they are truly, truly notorious, if they are Syrian citizens, they want them to return, they are so intent on reconstructing the fabric of Syrian society and culture. They don't want to leave hurts and animosities that they can avoid. I find a little difficulty accepting that because of my military background, but I do somewhat admire them for at least attempting to do that.

**Wertz:** It somewhat reminds one of Abraham Lincoln's policy.

**Black:** It does; it does. And the idea, had he survived, it was clear at Appomattox he had given instructions that you are to treat the South with dignity, and that Robert E. Lee would be treated with complete dignity, and that I'm sure did not just originate with General Grant. I'm sure that that was coordinated with the White House, and that it was President Lincoln himself who said, "We are going to bind the wounds that afflict this nation," and I think, had he lived, I think we would have much more effectively resolved the Civil War. We would not have had the terrible period of Reconstruction.

## Winning the War—and Civilian Casualties

**Wertz:** The Foreign Minister of Russia today, Mr. Lavrov, said that the situation in East Aleppo is in no way different than the situation currently in the city of Mosul, in Iraq; and I was just wondering,—although obviously there is a double standard in terms of the western countries on this issue,— I was just wondering what you think about that.

**Black:** Well it's interesting. In Mosul we are liberators. Just tonight I think CNN was reporting that the conditions for civilians were a catastrophe. Well, the fact of the matter is that when you fight an urban war, civilians will be killed. It is inevitable and it is inescapable; and rather than face that, with what the Syrians and the Russians were handling in Aleppo, we acted as though they were somehow doing something that was terrible.

Here we are in Mosul, and we are finding that we have precisely the same problems—that there are civilians who are dying, they are innocent civilians just like they are innocent civilians in Aleppo; and we have two alternatives, and this is what you face in urban combat. Either you can surrender and say, "We simply won't accept any civilian casualties," or you can simply pray and say, "God help them. We will try to kill as few as we possibly can, but we have got to win this war."

It has amazed me. I've looked at the figures. They've said that within—this is the Syrian Observatory for Human Rights; they said there have been 300 civilians killed in the Aleppo pocket in the last month. I find that figure to be stunningly low. I will tell you I fought in Viet Nam; I was a forward air-controller. I flew helicopters, but then I was on the ground as a forward air-controller, and I dropped bombs. Well, the Viet Cong chose to fight from villages, and in Viet Nam, throughout the war, we were killing 300 civilians every day. And here they are, they have very carefully targeted, they have taken tremendous casualties, the Syrians and their allies, trying to reduce the number of civilian casualties, and they have. They have been very successful. If you look at the overall casualties throughout the war, most casualties have been the Syrian Army or the rebels; and then a smaller portion, I don't know what the percentage would be, whether it would be 25%, have been civilians, but it is a remarkably low portion of the casualties, and this is, I'm relying on pro-rebel figures, not on government figures. It has been amazing, and I think we are going to find in Mosul that we are not going to take Mosul without civilian casualties.

There are going to be a lot of them, and I don't blame our government, I don't blame the Iraqi government: it is simply the nature of urban combat.

## Re-building Syria

**Wertz:** When we started this discussion, you made reference to the need to rebuild Syria, and General Flynn recently called for a Marshall Plan for northern Africa and the Middle East. I know that a few weeks ago there were a number of heads of private firms in Russia who were in Syria as part of a delegation there to discuss reconstruction there and keeping the economy of Syria—they have been denied two of their exports, grain and oil—so basically the idea was to really begin this process of rebuilding. The Chinese have also had a presence in Syria, which has not been so visible, but of course what the Russians and the Chinese have been working on is essentially the One-Belt-One-Road policy of China and the Eurasian Economic Union of Russia; and it is very clear that there is going to be a big need for reconstruction of Syria, but actually of the entire area.

**Black:** It's going to be huge. We have destroyed it. We went into Libya; Libya at the time we went in, was our closest ally in the war on terror. They had the highest per capita income of any North African country. We went in and under the guise of a no-fly zone, we bombed them into the Stone Age. They essentially have no government today. At one point in the last year or so, their parliament had to meet on a ship offshore because they couldn't control a ten-acre plot of land. They're absolutely in anarchy; there is no government.

We did that; we did that to them. They were highly successful before that. We have gone into Syria; we have created just gargantuan destruction in there. Had we not initiated the war in Syria, there would not have been a war in Syria. It was the United States who first decided, under Hillary Clinton, that we were going to go in, we were going to destroy Libya, capture their weapons, ship them to Turkey and across the border into Syria.

Under Ambassador Ford, who was there—and he was working with the French Ambassador—when there were some demonstrations he broke diplomatic protocol, and he worked his way in to talk to the demonstrators, and he assured them that we were with them. And he turned ordinary demonstrations into a revolution. From that time on we have poured billions of dollars— we're training terrorists in Jordan, in Saudi Arabia, in Qatar and in Turkey. These are people, we give them

*Aleppo before the civil war.*

basic training and then they go into the market, some of them to ISIS some of them to Al-Qaeda, some of them to other places.

We have done this destruction: we have trained them in how to blow down bridges, how to blow apart buildings, how to destroy things. No country on earth, including China, has the economic wherewithal to do the reconstruction that we do, and no country has the moral imperative to reconstruct like we do. The first thing we need to do is we need to drop the sanctions on them. Right now our sanctions actually prevent them from getting prosthetic devices; it prevents elderly people from receiving cancer medications. This is through the way that we manipulate the financial structure. It's a very cruel type of sanction that hurts innocent people. We need to get rid of the sanctions.

We have a mission that operates in Washington, DC. It's run by the terrorists and they lobby Congress for money to get weapons to go over and kill people. We need to shut down that mission immediately. At the same time, we need to establish a mission for the legitimate government of Syria in the United States. We have been so cautious of allowing anyone to have a voice on Syria that the UN Ambassador to Syria, Ambassador [Bashar] Al-Jaafari, has been restricted, and they say he cannot travel more than 25 miles from the UN. Why isn't he out on college campuses? Why isn't he facing hard questions where people could say, what about this, what about this? We're supposed to be a nation that loves free speech, and yet we have cut off every bit of free speech. We will not allow them.

Before the election in 2014, what did we do? We knew what the election outcome would be if Syrian expatriates were allowed to vote in the United States. We shut down the Embassy! And we got western countries all over to do it because we'd have had an enormous black eye, because what would the Syrians have done? They'd have voted overwhelmingly for President Bashar Al-Assad. We didn't want this. So we have censored this war in a way that is disturbing to me that our government has the power to be so ham-handed in its censorship. But we need to do those things. We need to begin to coordinate with the Syrian armed forces. American forces, American generals need to be talking to Syrian generals, and they need to be in the same room with Russian generals figuring out, where do we go, what do you need, how can we eliminate this last pocket, how can we bring peace? We need to be peacemakers, not war makers. We have a Department of Defense, not a Department of War which we did have long ago, and we need to revert to defense, and not to the creation of war throughout the world.

## A 'Time of Tremendous Hope'

**Wertz:** As you know, in Palmyra, once it was liberated, the Russians sponsored a concert in the same location where ISIS had beheaded residents of Palmyra. In a certain sense that was emblematic of two different conceptions of man, a completely bestial notion of man which the terrorists hold, and those who support the terrorists effectively hold, versus a conception of man which really is inspiring because you can just hear the work of Bach spreading throughout, not only the city, but throughout the desert and throughout the world.

**Black:** You had a solo violinist playing and sounds of that drifted over the desert and here he was in an amphitheater with columns around it. While I was there, I had the honor of shaking the hand of the man whose father had been beheaded because he refused to disclose the location of hidden antiquities which ISIS wanted very badly, so that they could ship them to the Turks, and the Turks would market them throughout the world to greedy oligarchs who wanted some piece of world history hanging in their study where they could look at it as they sipped their cocktails. And I shook the hand of this man and I said, "You know what? A thousand years from now when people come to Palmyra to look at this architectural gem, they're going to hear about your father and how he preserved the antiquities that they are seeing in Palmyra."

I think that we have a time of tremendous hope, a time of rebuilding of this great country. I think Syria has the opportunity to be great again. It is truly—I'm very religious—to me it is a miracle from God that a country of 23 million has managed to be cohesive and has faced NATO, the U.S., France, Britain, Turkey, Qatar, Saudi Arabia, all of the world's powers, the enormous power, and they've been descended on. Tens of thousands of jihadist mercenaries have been sent in and yet they have remained resolute, they love their President, they love their army, they despise the terrorists, and they consider every rebel to be a terrorist.

So I think the coming year is going to be very exciting for us, Will, and I think we are going to see great things happen. I think we are going to see an end to the Bush-Obama doctrine of regime change, and we are going to see a time when the world, perhaps, will see peace. This now, as you know, is the fifteenth anniversary of war for the United States. We have fought 15 continuous years of war. We have been bombing Iraq, believe it or not, for a quarter of a century, intermittently, but off and on we have dropped a third of a million bombs on Iraq, a country which never took any aggressive action towards us, a nation which never harbored terrorists, and yet here we are after 25 years, we are dropping bombs and we're killing people in Iraq. It's just amazing the failure of American elites to comprehend the complexity of foreign policy. There has been a void that is remarkable and I think almost a historic void in our comprehension of other cultures and other civilizations. I think that it's long time that we wrapped it up and took a different direction, and I think we're going to do that.

**Wertz:** I saw recently a report that over 25,000 Syrian children had entered the second stage of the Science Olympiad and that basically there was going to be another round, and then the finalist would participate in the international Science Olympiad which will occur next year; but it really hit me—here in the middle of this war, of this terror that has been visited upon this people—you still have children who are engaging in science projects and can compete internationally in this Olympiad. And I just think what you were saying in terms of the fact that this small country has stood up—I think instead of people vilifying Assad, they should be grateful for him, because if he hadn't stood up, think of the world we would be confronted with.

**Black:** If he hadn't stood up, Lebanon would have fallen, Jordan would have fallen, Israel would have been confronted with ISIS and Al-Qaeda, and instead of people with knives going out and committing acts, they'd have had 40 armored vehicles rush the gates and explode themselves; they'd have had divisions of Al-Qaeda troops pouring across the border, and who knows what that would have brought. We would have seen Turkey mobilize, once they had the Caliphate behind them, they would have begun to move towards Europe already. Erdogan has brought into question the treaty of 1923 that establishes the demarcation line between what is Europe and what is Turkey. Potentially we would have seen the loss of Europe, Western Europe, Eastern Europe, and so we have dodged a bullet despite ourselves. I think it is time that with the new President, I think a Marshall Plan would be a wonderful thing, and I think we owe it to the Syrians. We need to put our faults behind us; we don't need to dwell too much on them, but we need to restore order to the Middle East, and I think we're going to do it.

Will, thank you very much for being here tonight, I've enjoyed it very much.

**Wertz:** Thank you Senator. It's good seeing you.

# Every Day Counts In Today's Showdown To Save Civilization

That's why you need EIR's **Daily Alert Service**, a strategic overview compiled with the input of Lyndon LaRouche, and delivered to your email 5 days a week.

The election of Donald Trump to the Presidency of the Untied States has launched a new global era whose character has yet to be determined. The Obama-Clinton drive toward confrontation with Russia has been disrupted--but what will come next?

Over the next weeks and months there will be a pitched battle to determine the course of the Trump Administration. Will it pursue policies of cooperation with Russia and China in the New Silk Road, as the President-Elect has given some signs of? Will it follow through against Wall Street with Glass-Steagall?

The opposition to these policies will be fierce. If there is to be a positive outcome to this battle, an informed citizenry must do its part--intervening, educating, inspiring. That's why you need the EIR Daily Alert more than ever.

---

**TUESDAY, NOVEMBER 22, 2016**

Volume 3, Number 65

### EIR Daily Alert Service

P.O. Box 17390, WASHINGTON, DC 20041-0390

- Only Global Solutions, Based on New Principles, Can Work
- Tulsi Gabbard Meets with Donald Trump Regarding Syria
- Robert Kagan Throws in the Towel, Complains U.S. Is Becoming 'Solipsistic'
- War Party Moving To Preempt Trump-Putin Reset
- Syrian Army Makes More Progress in Aleppo
- Duterte Gives OK to Nuclear Power for Philippines
- Europe Will Suffer from Maintaining Russia Sanctions
- Former Chilean Diplomat Confirmed, 'We Will Joyfully Welcome Xi Jinping'
- Duterte and Putin Establish Philippines-Russia Cooperation
- François Fillon, Pro-Russian Thatcherite, Wins First Round of French Right-Wing Presidential Primary

### EDITORIAL

Only Global Solutions, Based on New Principles, Can Work

---

# Hamilton's Controversial Ally Dunlap: Opponent of Slavery, Defender of Progress

by Renée Sigerson

Decc.5—In recent discussions, American statesman Lyndon LaRouche has challenged those who desire great progress to result from the new, oncoming U.S. Presidency to recognize that the fight to achieve that goal is in fact part of an international battle for "a new universe of mankind." The world is at a pivotal point of transformation, in which human progress in any number of locations will come from upward shifts in human cognitive development overall, based on the drive for fundamental discoveries. That effect, which in human history has always required an interplay between classical principles of artistic composition and scientific discovery, will largely determine whether the new Administration in the U.S., and future administrations, will bring benefit to mankind.

In an earlier, immensely uncertain time, Alexander Hamilton recognized that it was the moral and cognitive development of early Americans which had to be deliberately promoted, if his economic policies, launched for progress against British-centered imperialism, would succeed. As we documented in the December 2 *EIR*, that is why Hamilton worked with stage director and painter William Dunlap to build the Park Theater in Manhattan, to provide New Yorkers with more access to improved, quality performances of great classical theater. As we document, it came to pass that the process of achieving that goal depended upon linking up with international theater projects out of Ger-

*William Dunlap, self-portrait circa 1812.*

many, and their radiating effects in Russia, for the effort to work.

Here we will say a few more things about William Dunlap personally, not merely because his collaboration with Hamilton has been "written out" of modern historical accounts. Our brief footnote here defends the Hamilton-Dunlap project against the charges of academic "experts" who insist that Dunlap was a "hack," whose terrible theater productions were typical of the "primitive," "low-level" early American outpouring of non-artistic "stock" or "stereotyped" theater productions which have no significance for what such "experts" call "culture."

Fortunately, there exists a small circle of American theater historians, typified by author Prof. Samuel Shanks of Iowa and Minnesota, that rejects this characterization wholesale. In an article entitled "Rooting Out Historical Mythologies: William Dunlap's 'A Trip to Niagara' and its Sophisticated Nineteenth Century Audience," Shanks identifies Dunlap accurately as a patriot who had a deep understanding of the unique mindset forming in the culturally complex multi-cultural American environment. The citizens of the newly formed nation were faced with the revolutionary challenge to persist in building a functional existence, largely out of nothing, as they struggled to free themselves, sometimes in what may have seemed clumsy fashion, from ingrained prejudices about the nature of man which still manifested itself in slavery and hierarchical social habits.

## The Battle Against Slavery

First and foremost, like Hamilton, Dunlap was an ardent opponent of slavery: he freed his family's slaves immediately following his father's death, was actively involved, as Hamilton had been, in the Manumission Society, and served as a trustee of the Free School for African Children. His much-maligned play, "Trip to Niagara," performed in 1828, one year after New York passed legislation finally eradicating slavery, was in part shaped to celebrate this victory over the slave system.

The play involves a "boatload" of characters both from

*"Distant View of Niagara Falls" by Thomas Cole, 1830.*

Europe and America, traveling up the Hudson against a moving "rolling-pin" stage background, showing the actual scenery on the Hudson's eastern bank. With humor, the play illuminates the contrast between British stodginess versus American commitment to progress. As Shanks convincingly demonstrates, Dunlap stuffed the play with endless contemporary references known to audiences of that time, evoking an audience reaction to events and personalities which typified that well-known difference. For example, in that context, clearly underlining his own well-known determination that slavery be ended, Dunlap introduced a character named Job Jerryson, the first-ever portrayal of a free African-American brought on to the American stage. Job, according to Shanks, was most likely named, per the Biblical reference, to emphasize the incredible struggle of African-Americans to survive the nightmares of slavery; at a critical moment in the play, he declares: "Master! – I have no master. Master indeed…. I am my own master."

This commitment to eradicate slavery was central to Dunlap's collaboration with Hamilton when they first met back in the 1790s. When Hamilton arranged for over 100 New Yorkers to buy shares in Dunlap's Park Theater (see Dec. 2 article), the participants included Hamilton's closest friends, all of whom were involved

in the Manumission Society, namely: Stephen Van Rensselaer, a New York gubernatorial candidate; James Watson, his running mate; William Bayard, the man who took Hamilton home after he had been shot by Aaron Burr, and in whose arms Hamilton died; DeWitt Clinton, the individual most responsible for the building of the Erie Canal; Nathaniel Fish, named as the executor of Hamilton's will; and Rufus King, Hamilton's closet political ally.

One year after Hamilton's death, Dunlap went bankrupt. The Park Theater was subsequently taken over by an explicitly pro-British Theater crowd, who derided the popular, American-authored productions which Dunlap would include on the stage, along with classical productions. The American theater works merely reflected the population's strong attachment to stories of the 1776 Revolution. In 1826, a competitor to the now Anglophile Park Theater was opened under the name Bowery Theater, financed by three prominent descendants, namely the sons of President James Monroe, of John Jacob Astor (whose operations in the Pacific Basin put him in the center of U.S. relations with Russia), and of Alexander Hamilton. This is where Dunlap's "Trip to Niagara" was presented, with great acclamation from the anti-British section of the New York population, in 1828.

### Cole, Cooper, and the Erie Canal

Dunlap was also a close personal friend of author James Fenimore Cooper, whose beautifully written fictional accounts of American life are equally derided today by "politically correct" critics, who consider his characters "psychologically flat," and even, in the case of Native Americans and African-American servants, "stereotyped to the point of being racist." Contrary to such academic judgment, the reality was that Dunlap and Cooper were an absolute backbone in the fight to eradicate slavery, and to promote human dignity. Another theme which his theater works emphasized was American rejection of the typical British obsession with "deference" as a right of the upper strata in society when dealing with lower classes.

Dunlap, along with painter Thomas Cole, was a member of James Fenimore Cooper's "Bread and Cheese Club," a weekly luncheon affair where writers and artists would meet. Dunlap, who had resumed painting in the later years of his life, was also a member, with Cole, of the New York Drawing Association, which met three times a week for drawing sessions. The play "Trip to Niagara" was also designed by Dunlap to promote Cole who had become renowned for his landscapes of the Hudson River in a variety of weather conditions, and receiving sunlight at different times of the day. The moving, "roller-pin" like diorama moving in the background portrayed exactly the route Cole had taken between Manhattan and the Catskill Mountains when he painted his most recently famous works.

Derided today by "theater historians" as undeserving of serious attention, "Trip to Niagara" drew a highly political audience of enthusiasts who supported the just-completed Erie Canal and promoted Fenimore Cooper's novels. There occurred in the Bowery Theater a surge of theater attendance that was unprecedented. At a time when most theater productions were held once a month, 17 performances of "Trip to Niagara" were sold out the first month it was shown, with people still standing outside after the 3,500 seats were filled.

For today's purposes, the account of Dunlap's collaboration with Hamilton and his subsequent work serves as an inviting illustration of the principle that the social development of the human mind through classical art is a necessary component of the fight for economic progress and justice.

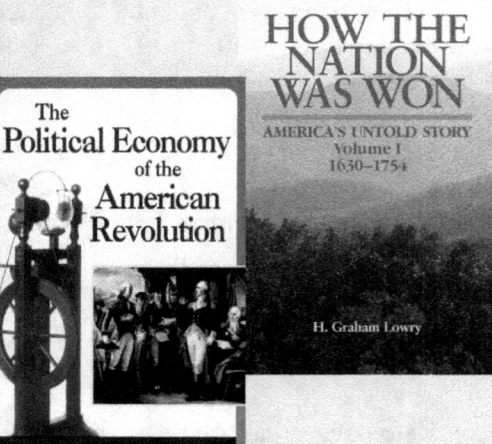

# Alexander Hamilton: To Stimulate 'the Best Minds and the Best Spirits'

*The following excerpt is taken from the December 1 LaRouchePAC Fireside Chat, featuring EIR Economics Editor Paul Gallagher.*

**Question:** Hello, this is N. in Oakland. I've got a question going back to Hamilton, and I'm not certain whether he speaks of it in the *Report on the National Bank* or [the] manufacturers report, but in one of those documents he writes this explicitly in opposition to the Secretary of State Thomas Jefferson and the Attorney General [Edmund] Randolph. And what I'm curious, is there a statement specifically from Jefferson relative to his insistence that the United States stay an agricultural land-mass, an agricultural country as opposed to manufacturing, as Hamilton has prescribed and was arguing for? So that's a specific question; is it clear?

**Gallagher:** It's clear, but there wasn't that opposition in the case—it wasn't really that kind of opposition. Hamilton was not saying "we must be a manufacturing country," while Jefferson was saying, "we must be an agricultural country." Jefferson's understanding of agriculture was slave-cotton agriculture. He idealized—I don't want to get deeply into Jefferson, but essentially his opposition, you can see it in the famous Virginia Resolutions that he wrote; his opposition was to the disruption of the free trade arrangements which then existed between British manufacture, and American both tobacco and increasing cotton, slave agriculture.

Obviously, Hamilton's plan inclusively was a direct campaign against slavery. He himself, along with Ben Franklin, they were the founders of the Manumission Society and the chief organizers for the abolition of slavery before and after the Constitution was adopted. And inclusively that's part of his drive for productivity: Hamilton, while he was an aide to Washington, in the middle of the Revolutionary War, was already corresponding with the Morrises and others saying: What we need is a bank, and we need a bank in order to bring together the capital, the savings of the country and place in the hands of those who could make the most productive use of it; and such a bank which constitutes a cooperation between the productive efforts of the govern-ment and those of the individual farmers, entrepreneurs, artisans, that's what we need a bank for, is to bring those together, as he kept saying, "so as to direct the capital into the hands of those who could put it to the most productive use." And in particular to the most inventive use, so there were breakthroughs and the use of the mind, the stimulation of the mind in doing that. Obviously, that encompassed both agriculture, progress in agriculture, and also in manufacturing, which Hamilton was in the middle of, bringing skilled artisans over from Scotland in order to develop new industries, new manufacturing in the United States; he did that personally.

So that's, I think, the way to understand it, not as in any way an opposition between a bank for manufactures and a bank for agriculture; or a desire for an agricultural country as opposed to a desire for a manufacturing country. It was a desire for an inventive and productive country above all others, which Hamilton thought the new country could become.

So, it's a surprise, when we organize, it's a surprise to people that there was such an idea for a national credit institution with that purpose. And they've never heard anything like that, they've never heard anything about such a design for a bank, and yet, they hear now about Alexander Hamilton, they hear all kinds of nonsense about him, but they've never heard anything like that. We have to make that common knowledge. And let Jefferson take care of himself. Let his ghost take care of itself. ...

Hamilton was one of the very few founders of the Society for the Promotion of Useful Manufactures in the United States; but don't forget he was also, with Franklin, the founder of the Manumission Society and they waged a real fight and came fairly close to a Constitutional abolition of slavery before they didn't prevail. So, it was the question of the primacy of invention, of innovation, "the stimulation of the best minds and the best spirits," was the way Hamilton talked about it. And the use of a bank, with cooperation both to be a liaison between the government and private banks, of which there were very few and he wanted to see many more created; and also as he kept saying in his correspondence, to place savings, capital, "in the hands of those who can put it to the most productive use."

# III. Mankind's Future

### RUSSIA AND CHINA RELY ON CREATIVITY

# Can Zero Be a Negative Quantity? Yes, If It Is a Zero-Deficit Budget!

by Helga Zepp-LaRouche, chairwoman of the German Civil Rights Solidarity Movement party (BüSo)

Dec. 3—Every day it becomes more obvious that there are two utterly opposed global paradigms that determine the behavior of nations. While opposition to the bankrupt paradigm of globalization becomes stronger and stronger in the trans-Atlantic world, and the Establishment tries to hold on to it ever more doggedly, the nations cooperating with the New Silk Road—with increasing clarity—are committed to the creativity of their peoples and to cooperation on the common aims of mankind.

The Western politicians and media who are accustomed to seeing Russian President Putin only through the lens of demonization, would do well to read through Putin's December 1st State of the Nation address before the Russian Federal Assembly, without prejudice, for once. Since the rejection of Obama— because Hillary Clinton's defeat was also that—and the first telephone conversations that Donald Trump had with Vladimir Putin and Xi Jinping, a real opportunity for normalizing relations among the world's three most important nations has opened up. And only a suicidal fool would throw away this opportunity.

If we take into account the entire chronology of Putin's offers to the West—including his hopeful address to the German Bundestag in 2001 and his speech to the Munich Security Conference in 2007 expressing his keen disappointment—then we should accept his words at face value when he says, "We do not want confrontation with anyone. We have no

need for it ... We do not seek and never have sought enemies. We need friends. But we will not allow our interests to be infringed upon or ignored."

Later on in his speech Putin stressed—as priorities for the educational system—the fostering of knowledge and morality as the prerequisite for the viability of society. The interest of young people in national Classical literature, culture, and history must be awakened, he said. The schools must promote creativity, by the children learning to think independently, and learning to work both on their own and as part of a team, to master exceptional challenges and formulate and reach goals. Admittedly, gifted education is important, he said, but in principle, the educational system must be based on

Xinhua

*Thousands of Greek retirees rally in central Athens, against the fresh round of pension cuts implemented by the government under bailout agreements.*

*Vladimir Putin addressed the Primakov Readings International Forum in Moscow, November 30, 2016.*

the understanding that all children and teenagers are gifted, and can achieve success in science, the creative fields, and life. The task of the state is to foster their talents.

Putin also underscored the fundamental importance of basic research as the basis for economic growth and social progress. More than 200 laboratories have already been established, he said, that are in a position to operate on the global level, thanks to very large subsidies, and which are led by scientists who have identified the trends in global scientific developments. In this connection, he said, it is also important to overcome the bottlenecks which have existed in Russia since the time of the czars by utilizing these scientific advances in the production of commercial goods.

The Putin demonizers should also study the speech Putin gave the day before at the Primakov Readings International Forum, held in honor of Yevgeni Primakov, the former prime minister and "intellectual pioneer" who died 18 months ago. U.S.-Russian relations were also high on the agenda of his speech. Putin referred to Primakov's belief that it would be very difficult to adequately address today's big challenges—especially in the fight against terrorism in the Middle East—"without a serious partnership between Russia and the United States." Primakov, according to the Russian President, "had the truly strategic vision" that allowed him to "look into the future and see how unviable and one-sided" was the model of a unipolar world. It was Primakov, Putin said, who first advocated trilat-

eral cooperation among Russia, China, and India, which then evolved into the BRICS, "which is gaining weight and influence in the world." Moreover, Primakov's insistence on maintaining close ties with partners in the Commonwealth of Independent States (CIS), Putin said, "is the backbone of our integration policy in Eurasia … We hope that talks with our partners, including those on linking up with China's Silk Road Economic Belt project, will enable us to build a grand Eurasian partnership."

## The Inalienable Right to Development

Another document which the geopolitically minded western politicians and media should study, is a new White Paper by the Chinese government titled, "The Right to Development: China's Philosophy, Practice and Contribution," which affirms that there is an "inalienable right" for all peoples and countries to develop. "The right to development must be enjoyed and shared by all peoples. Realizing the right to development is the responsibility of all countries and also the obligation of the international community," the paper says. "It requires governments of all countries to formulate development strategies and policies suited to their own realities, and it requires concerted efforts of the international community as a whole. China calls on all countries to pursue equal, open, all-round and innovative common development; it promotes inclusive development, and creates conditions for all peoples to share the right to development."

But the white paper goes much further. It clearly shows that China's model for development and China's political and social structure has achieved unqualified success. And while the model continues to develop, it is at a pace and in a form that is determined by the Chinese people themselves. The paper notes that China has already raised 700 million people out of poverty, now with only 5.7% of the population living under the poverty line, making it the first nation, the report notes, to reach the UN's Millennium Goals. But China is determined to eliminate poverty altogether. The Chinese government outlined a strategy for entirely eliminating poverty among the rural population by 2020 in its "Outline of the 13th Five-Year Program for the National Economic and Social Development of the People's Republic of China," published in March 2016.

New China TV

*Caterpillar Chairman and CEO Doug Oberhelman sees the Belt and Road possibly as much as "a 50-year project that will open up a tremendous amount of economic growth through Eurasia."*

## 'A New Wave of Prosperity'

Anyone who does not want to listen to Putin or China can study a white paper by the heavy equipment company Caterpillar, builder of machines for construction, recently reported on in Chinese media, on the significance of the Belt and Road Initiative.[1] This initiative will unleash "a new wave of prosperity" for China and the rest of the world, it says. The construction of an infrastructure network—one of the initiative's priorities—will make possible the free flow and efficient utilization of resources, market integration, and coordination of economic policy among nations.

The construction of the infrastructure will help lower the costs of logistics, boost the competitiveness of the emerging economies, and reduce inequality among nations. Caterpillar considers the "Belt and Road" initiative to be an "open and inclusive" framework which will permit all the countries along the routes to participate in construction of the project. "It is not intended as, and cannot be, a solo effort of China," according to the white paper.

Caterpillar values the business opportunities opened by the initiative, and hopes to be able to participate even more in projects along the routes, explained Chen

1. Xinhua, "Belt and Road Initiative Presents 'Enormous Opportunity': Caterpillar," Nov. 30, 2016: http://english.cctv.com/2016/11/30/ART-InmTMtudylbAMdCXsUfBJ161130.shtml/. Caterpillar Chairman and CEO Doug Oberhelman had expressed this optimism in speaking with New China TV in September 2015: https://www.youtube.com/watch?v=y1SQ8Phput4/.

Qihua, Caterpillar's Vice-President and Chairman of Caterpillar China.

Moreover, western politicians and media should finally realize that there is broad support in the population for international cooperation, especially in the area of scientific and technological progress. The Citizens' Dialogue of the European Space Agency (ESA), which has 22 member states, revealed that 88 percent of those it surveyed support the agency's space program, and 96% are convinced that space offers opportunities that do not exist on Earth, but should be pursued.

In his report on this survey at the "Frieslandmahl" celebration at Upjever Air Base, former German astronaut Thomas Reiter, now chief ESA coordinator of International Space Station Affairs, said there is reason to be optimistic in spite of the endless budget controversies at the European level. The EU8 billion spent on the space program during the past five years, he said, have generated EU14.5 billion in economic benefits for Europe and its citizens.

"But there is also the political aspect of international cooperation. This works well in spite of the conflicts on Earth," Reiter said. "There are 95 countries taking part in the ISS research work, and up there the objectives are for the good of all mankind."

Reiter was also optimistic about the lunar dimension of space development, particularly on the far side of the Moon. It may serve as a launch site for deep space missions in the future.

Bernhard von Weyhe, head of the Communications Department of the European Space Operations Center in Darmstadt, Germany, also addressed the "bridge function" that space technology serves for mankind in an interview with the *Allgemeine Zeitung*. He said that "joint manned space projects promote human solidarity, even at the time of the Cold War. Space has always been an area for intensive international collaboration—and it continues to act as a bridge. Space travel is *per se* a project of cooperation."

The common denominator for all of these statements is this: Mankind's future lies in nations cooperating for the economic development of the entire world, and for the common aims of mankind, especially in the development of technology, science, and human creativity. It is well worth investing in such cooperation. Whoever does not understand this, and instead sets his sights on a zero-deficit budget, will end up empty-handed.

# Italy: The Third Shock

by Claudio Celani

Dec. 7—This time, the earthquake with its epicenter in Italy was a political one, and is sending shockwaves globally. On Dec. 4, Italian voters overwhelmingly rejected a constitutional reform bill that would have enslaved them once and forever to a foreign dictatorship centered in the European Union (EU). This is the third shock, after Brexit and the electoral defeat of Obama/Hillary Clinton, delivered by the worldwide revolt of the forgotten citizen against a political establishment responsible for an economic crisis and wars which are driving millions of people into poverty, despair and death.

Not by chance, the highest percentages of "No" votes in the Dec. 4 national referendum came from southern regions, such as Sicily and Sardinia, which have the highest rates of youth unemployment and poverty, and from the northeastern region of Veneto, the hardest hit by the post-2008 industrial desertification and a high rate of suicide among small industrialists. With voter participation of nearly 70% domestically (66% when voters abroad are included), Italians gave a lesson in wisdom by rejecting 60-40 a Constitutional reform dictated by the EU and by investment bankers. The aim of the reform, as stated in the introduction to the bill, was "to exhaustively rationalize the complex multilevel system of governance, articulated among the European Union, the state, and local autonomies." No less than four new Constitutional Articles would have established EU law as on the same level as Italian constitutional law.

The Italian Parliament had approved Prime Minister Matteo Renzi's constitutional reform with a simple majority, corresponding to the government's parliamentary majority. Italy's Constitution prescribes that constitutional changes need approval in a national referendum if a two-third majority is not achieved in Parliament.

As Professor Luciano Barra Caracciolo, an active member of Italy's judiciary branch and author of the political blog "Orizzonti48," explained to *EIR*, the reform was aimed at "transposing" onto a constitutional level "European policies," i.e., "a political direction shaped abroad, in a Brussels dominated by financial

wikimedia commons

*Italian voters overwhelmingly rejected a constitutional reform dictated by the European Union and by investment bankers.*

and oligopolistic lobbies, independent of any electoral result in Italy. This especially concerned the so-called 'guidelines' and the 'resolutions,' by the Commission and the EU Council. It was a far-reaching constitutional change, 'unique in Europe.'"

Along with this unprecedented suppression of national sovereignty in its own constitution, the Italian parliamentary system would have been turned into a mere notarial function for decisions taken by the executive branch, which, in turn, would only be a transmission belt for Brussels "guidelines."

In fact, one of the two chambers, the Senate, would be suppressed and replaced by a smaller body composed of a selection of regional legislators and mayors. In the scale of political corruption, regional legislators are at the top of the list, but they would now be granted immunity. The Senate would no longer be allowed to vote on no-confidence motions against the government, nor vote on the budget, but it would vote on international treaties and participate in "decisions aimed at shaping and implementing European Union legislative acts and policies."

No less than four articles of the proposed new Constitution (55, 70, 80, and 117), for the first time mention Italy's membership in the European Union, and put EU law at the same level as Constitutional law. In total, Renzi's reform would have changed 47 Articles of the Constitution.

The introduction of "EU Law" in an explicit form in the Italian constitution, would ensure that, even while provisions for the General Welfare remained, the latter could be totally and "legally" violated by Acts of the European Union, which the Constitutional Court could no longer challenge, because they have the same force as Constitutional Law. This would have made possible what JP Morgan had advocated in a 2013 paper: namely, that "socialistic" features of Constitutions in some European countries, especially in Southern Europe, should be eliminated or neutralized.

"The constitutions and political settlements in the southern periphery, put in place in the aftermath of the fall of fascism, have a number of features which appear to be unsuited to further integration in the region," the report said. "The political systems in the periphery were established in the aftermath of dictatorship, and were defined by that experience. Constitutions tend to show a strong socialist influence, reflecting the political strength that left wing parties gained after the defeat of

Xinhua/Jin Yu

*Italian Prime Minister Matteo Renzi announced his resignation Dec. 5, 2016, as the Sunday referendum overwhelmingly rejected his constitutional reforms.*

fascism. Political systems around the periphery typically display several of the following features: weak executives; weak central states relative to regions; constitutional protection of labor rights; consensus-building systems which foster political clientelism; and the right to protest if unwelcome changes are made to the political status quo."

The JP Morgan paper is strikingly consistent with the substance of Renzi's reform. Someone has even said that the reform was written in such bad Italian, that it might have been translated from English. In order to ensure that "the right to protest" be neutralized, the Renzi reform was coupled with an electoral law which would give a parliamentary majority bonus to any party that achieves 40% of the vote in the first run, or comes first with any number of votes in the second run. Thus, a party with, say, 20% of the national vote could end up in gaining 55% of the seats in the new Chamber, the only legislative body now entitled to vote confidence in the executive. This electoral bill has been compared to the 1923 "Legge Acerbo," the law that allowed Mussolini to gain a majority in the Parliament.

Furthermore, the candidates elected to the Chamber of Deputies would not be chosen by the voters, but by the party leadership: it would not be possible to vote for a single candidate, but only for the entire slate. The party decides who is on top and who is on bottom of the slate, therefore deciding who gets elected and who does not.

The combination of the constitutional reform and the electoral law would have created a monster, with a legislature *de facto* run by the executive, and the latter run by the party leadership. Totalitarianism anyone? Italy's political system as established by the 1948 Constitution—the first ever in the history of the Italian nation—has indeed been unbalanced in favor of the legislative, but Renzi's reform would have made it unbalanced in favor of the executive, and to a deadly extent. A real correction would be a reform in favor of a Presidential system, i.e. a real separation between the executive and the legislative powers. When the Constitutional Congress gathered after World War Two, Italy was coming out of Mussolini's dictatorship, and the Constitutional Fathers were concerned to create a political system that would hinder a repetition of the fascist dictatorship. Thus, they fell into the trap laid by the British, and adopted a pure parliamentary system, where the government is elected by Parliament (confidence vote) and can be toppled by Parliament any moment. This created great instability in government, with 50 governments over only 46 years (1948-1994). Things have slightly improved with the introductions of different electoral systems, but not decisively. Several attempts at constitutional reform have been made in the last decades, but they have all failed.

In 2014, Renzi decided to push through a reform which would turn a system which was unbalanced in favor of the legislative, into a system that is extremely unbalanced in favor of the executive. As James Madison wrote in the Federalist Papers (No. 47), "The accumulation of all powers, legislative, executive, and judiciary, in the same hands, whether of one, a few, or many, and whether hereditary, self-appointed, or elective, may justly be pronounced the very definition of tyranny."

Renzi decided to push through his tyrannical scheme even though he knew that he would split the country into two opposing sides. He trusted his demagogical capacity to sell his reform as something that would make the legislative process "quicker, cheaper and more modern," thus enabling him to make reforms that would ultimately bring more stability, more jobs, more healthcare, etc.

The question Italians were asked to answer with a "Yes" or a "No" is an unprecedented example of Goebbels-like manipulation. It said: "Do you approve the text of the Constitutional Law concerning 'Provisions to overcome parity Bicameralism, to reduce the number of members of Parliament, to contain the functioning costs of institutions, the suppression of CNEL and the revision of Chapter V of the Constitution?'" In other words, voters were asked whether they wanted to reduce the size and the costs of government institutions, suppress a consultative board (CNEL) made up of political, trade union and industrial representatives, and change a Constitutional provision (Chapter V) which transfers powers from regional administration to the central government,—without explaining in detail what this is about, and, especially, how this would be implemented. Nothing about the real aim of the reform, as laid out in the introduction to the text of the Parliamentary Act, is explained in the question which was printed on the ballot, and which Italians were supposed to answer with "Yes" or "No." However, Italians smelled foul and voted "No."

## What Happens Now

Contrary to what the EU bureaucrats and government leaders have said, they are in fact terribly frightened that as a consequence of the referendum vote, Renzi will ultimately be toppled and early elections called, which the M5S (Five Star Movement) will win and lead Italy out of the Euro. Although the M5S leadership has been ambiguous on the Euro, nevertheless the Euro and EU austerity policies have been up-front in the referendum campaign. Lega Nord leader Matteo Salvini has openly campaigned for leaving the Euro, and even Forza Italia leader and former Prime Minister Silvio Berlusconi has proposed a "parallel currency."

Although the opposition is calling for early elec-

*Initial market reaction to voter rejection of the EU and banker's Constitutional reform referendum in Italy.*

tions and even Renzi is favorable, it is not clear what will happen in the next weeks. On Sunday night, Renzi announced that he would resign the next day, but when he went to President Sergio Mattarella, Mattarella told him to go back to work. Mattarella told him to stay at least until the budget is approved. In order to do this quickly, Renzi is going to call a no-confidence vote on the budget. Thus, we will have the grotesque situation of a Prime Minister who wins a Parliamentary vote of confidence and then resigns!

However, Renzi, or whoever replaces him, must now face a turbulent situation in his own party, where he may not have the same consensus he has had so far,— along with a dramatic economic and social crisis. The most urgent issue he must deal with is the banking crisis. The Italian banking system has accumulated over EU200 billion of non-performing loans (NPL) as a result of ten years of economic depression induced by the 2008 crisis and by EU austerity policies. The system urgently needs a solution, and there is no way that the "market solution" suggested by the EU and the European Central Bank could work. The EU permits a government bailout only after a bail-in, i.e. a confiscation of shareholders', depositors' and bondholders' money.

After a partial implementation of the bail-in regulations in the case of four local banks at the end of 2015, which provoked a large political backlash, the Renzi government decided that this was not practicable, and has opposed the bail-in solution for other banks.

However, the bail-in ghost has come back to haunt Renzi and whoever might succeed him, urgently in the case of Monte dei Paschi di Siena (MPS), the oldest active bank in the world and considered to be a systemic bank. MPS is facing bankruptcy unless it succeeds in recapitalizing itself and getting rid of its NPL burden. The "market solution" pushed for MPS includes an EU5 billion recapitalization and the sale of EU27 billion of NPLs. Last July, an international consortium of banks, led by—guess whom—JP Morgan, stepped forward to finance the recapitalization. But two months later, the same consortium demanded a bail-in of the bondholders as a condition. Thus, two days after the Referendum, on Dec. 6, MPS announced that a successful "voluntary conversion" of EU1 billion in subordinate bonds had taken place *de facto*, a bail-in: bondholders exchange their bonds for shares, which become capital, but whose value could evaporate if anything goes wrong. And something will go wrong for sure.

Even after the bail-in, nobody believes that the capital increase and the NPL sale will be successful, so that in the end, the government will be forced to intervene with a bailout. The MPS case is only the most urgent one, but a series of large banks is next in line for recapitalization, as demanded by the European Banking Union standards.

There is no way "market solutions" could work, Only a national program, which includes banking separation, government recapitalization and a real investment plan, can turn the situation around. This involves leaving the Euro. If Italy, the third largest economy of the Eurozone, leaves the Euro, the Euro is finished.

The Euro is also finished if Italy stays in the Euro, but its banking crisis goes out of control. A full-fledged

*Professor Luciano Barra Caracciolo*

youtube grab

*Lega Nord leader Matteo Salvini*

Wikipedia

*M5S founder Beppe Grillo*

EIRNS

*Economist Nino Galloni*

Italian banking crisis will affect the global financial system, including megabanks such as JP Morgan and Deutsche Bank, which are filled with toxic derivative papers.

Renzi may be tempted into a flight forward into early elections, in order to escape decisions on the crisis. However, this would be very bad for the country, because he could be replaced by a technocratic government with no inhibitions against murderous austerity.

Economist Nino Galloni, a friend of Lyndon La-Rouche, gives Renzi some chance, "but he must change contents and alliances," Galloni said. Renzi had ear-lier made some good moves, Galloni said, such as fighting against the EU on the Italian budget to be able finance immigration and reconstruction costs, and his resistance against bail-ins. However, his push for the "counter-reformation" has swept him away.

The front that defeated Renzi, however, was united only on the "No" vote, but has conflicting political aims. The Lega Nord, for instance, is strongly anti-Euro but also anti-immigrant; Berlusconi's Forza Italia party is mildly anti-EU and neoliberal; and the Five Star Movement (M5S), which would probably win the elections if they were held today, is officially in favor of Glass-Steagall, but ambiguous on the EU and the Euro. Moreover, it is split between a jacobin/Malthusian party and a pro-growth national force.

On Dec. 5, Galloni, who is close to some M5S circles, launched an appeal to M5S founder Beppe Grillo and the M5S representatives to "elaborate a program of national defense and responsible development that can indicate an alternative path for everyone, and a way out of a situation which is socially, economically, financially and ethically more and more unsustainable."

The problem with the M5S came out clearly when Galloni was proposed to become the Finance Minister under the newly elected M5S Mayor of Rome, Virginia Raggi. After an internal fight, the Malthusians inside the M5S prevailed and rejected Galloni and his investment plan. Expect turbulent times for Italy and Europe.